# Gold Shoes

*graphic poetry by*

# Leanne Grabel

*Finishing Line Press*
Georgetown, Kentucky

# Gold Shoes

*A poem begins with a lump in the throat.*
Robert Frost
*As for sound, I live in one great bell of sound.*
William Stafford
*The visual way is to doodle a rectangle . . .*
Tom Wujek

Copyright © 2018 by Leanne Grabel
ISBN 978-1-63534-471-4 First Edition
All rights reserved under International and Pan-American Copyright Conventions.
No part of this book may be reproduced in any manner whatsoever without written permission from the publisher, except in the case of brief quotations embodied in critical articles and reviews.

## ACKNOWLEDGMENTS

These poems were published previously in these literary magazines:
"Toothpicks" and "Blame" *(The Opiate)*
"Gold Shoes" *(After Hour Review)*
"Assisted Living" *(Cloudbank)*
"Bees," "Wood Clothes," "Rules of Marriage"
   *(Drunk in a Midnight Choir)*
"A Little Hip," "Thicketry" and "Rules of Marriage"
   *(Riding Light)*
"Sheen" *(The Nervous Breakdown)*
"Sunday 4AM" *(Blue Lake Review)*
"Math Strain," "Flash" *(Badlands Literary Review)*
"Not Another Shoe Poem" *(Gobshite Quarterly—upcoming)*
"My Mother's Hair" *(VoiceCatcher)*
"The Lemon and the Lama" (Oregon Poetic Voices)
"Wound" (Oregon Poetic Voices)
"The Day My Mother Died"
   *(The Opiate Online & Cream City Review)*
"Felt," "Marital Clamp," "Romance," "My Husband and the German Judges," upcoming in *Broad Street*.

Publisher: Leah Maines

Editor: Christen Kincaid

Cover Art: Leanne Grabel

Author Photo: Leanne Grabel

Cover Design: Elizabeth Maines McCleavy

Printed in the USA on acid-free paper.
Order online: www.finishinglinepress.com
   also available on amazon.com

Author inquiries and mail orders:
Finishing Line Press
P. O. Box 1626
Georgetown, Kentucky 40324
U. S. A.

# Table of Contents

1. Pink .................................................................................. 1
Dewiness for Sale. Pre-Owned. In Box. ............................... 3
Gold Shoes ......................................................................... 4
Assisted Living ................................................................... 5
Hula-Hoop .......................................................................... 6

2. Red ................................................................................. 7
Toothpicks .......................................................................... 9
Day 33,002 ........................................................................ 10
Hat Story ........................................................................... 11
Marital Clamp ................................................................... 12
Rules of Marriage .............................................................. 13

3. Purple ........................................................................... 15
Flash .................................................................................. 16
Blame ................................................................................ 17
Piano Teacher .................................................................... 18

4. Brown ........................................................................... 19
German Judges ................................................................. 20
The Enemy Is My Age ....................................................... 21
Bees ................................................................................... 22
A Little Hip ....................................................................... 23

5. Blue .............................................................................. 25
Sheen ................................................................................. 26
Pinkie Ring ....................................................................... 27
The War of 2001 ............................................................... 29
Growing Smaller ............................................................... 30
Family Cruise After the Father ......................................... 31
Do Birds Fall in the Forest? .............................................. 32

6. Gray ............................................................................. 33
Math Strain ....................................................................... 34
Another Hair Poem ........................................................... 35
Romance ............................................................................ 36
Fresco ................................................................................ 37

7. Black .................................................................................39
Underarm Hair ....................................................................40
Tiny Writers .........................................................................41
Thicketry ..............................................................................43
My Generous Collar ............................................................44
Onus .....................................................................................45
Sunday 4 AM ......................................................................46

8. Green .................................................................................47
Wood Clothes .....................................................................48
Not Another Shoe Poem ...................................................49
Disclaimer ...........................................................................50
Felt .......................................................................................51

9. Yellow ................................................................................53
The Lemon and the Lama .................................................54
Personal Growth ................................................................55

10. The Day My Mother Died ............................................57

*to the
famiglia*

# 1. Pink

The wink and whisper. Glint. The grin. The blistered lip. The skin. Before the scar. And after. Feathers' scent. Tender's hue. Before the rub. The whip. The raw. Before the rough. The round. The sweets. Pulp as baby. Red as baby. Pain as baby.

**Dewiness for Sale. Pre-Owned. In Box.**

I aged last week. Hard. Time muscled past me so fast. No time for protection. No sunscreen. No hazard suit. You know what it's like. Dancing as fast as you can. And showing it. Clacking of wood marionettes. Hanging from monstrous gazebos. Scratches and cuts. Scratches and cuts. You have on a hat. But. Your skull swells. The hatband dug into me. Now. There's a divot. Over my eyebrows. Right where I rue. There are dozens of creases. And pleats. O. My neck. A plaid skirt. Like the trunk of a tree. (But resilient.) I tuck in my words. Yes. I store favorite phrases. And Dewiness. Crumpled. In creases. What's left of it. It isn't much. I'll never use it. Again. I rarely used it. To begin with. I should sell it. Craigslist. Or eBay. *Dewiness. Pre-Owned. In Box.* I've got the perfect box.

**Gold Shoes**

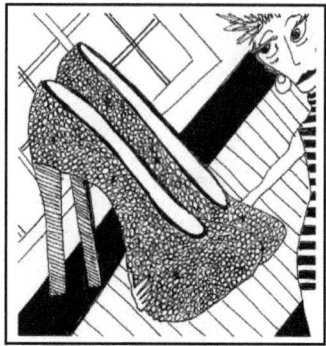

It was a dream. Of course. I'll keep it brief. I was sleeping on the rollaway. Assisted Living. Visiting my mother. And. You came to visit. You were naked. In the rollaway. We were *rolling*. I was naked. After years of inactive desire. At least for me. I was wrong. Not for you. I knew that. To begin with. A dream. Well. You hugged me. From behind. Around the breasts. I liked that. In the dream. You could tell. My face! O. O. Anyone could tell. I was naked. Not embarrassed. Not fat. Not a thought. (Well.) Embarrassed by my feet. Fists of gingerroot. Hairy rootstock. Then. Your daughter. The eldest. I liked her. She liked me. She was there. She was teaching. Apache beading. She was wearing gorgeous shoes. I loved them. They were gold. They had sparkle. I really needed those shoes. (To hide the gingerroot.) I kept asking. For the shoes. It was obnoxious. You left. So'd your daughter.

## Assisted Living

She wanted nothing on the walls. Assisted Living. *Not staying.* She insisted. Although actually. The place was lovely. Proud flowers. Kind fires. Burnished knobbery. All levels of care. But bad music. Like a pestilence. Or a throb. Another throb. Deep. Dim. Yet strangely exact. Like Time. Or Death. Scooting after them. As it were. In its sagging silver jumpsuit. It was careless. Change the music! My mother. 93. No biggie. Most were. Or 92. Or 96. A handful were100. They didn't brag. The others wondered. *Will I make it?* Most were hopeful. Some found love. New love. Was there sex? *Ask Sylvia.* I told my mother. She wouldn't do it. She'd had a stroke. A little singeing of the scaffold. A little melting of the bold. She wanted nothing on the walls. *I'm not staying.* My sister's boyfriend still brought in a painting. Red flowers. Green fern fronds. In an ornate gold frame. He hung the painting. Above the big blonde TV. I brought in tulips. Same red. Coincidental. Like persimmons. Enormous cherry trees. The size of buildings. Burst with blossoms. Out the windows. Pink as petticoats. And. The dining room. Elegant. Peach linens. Fancy napkin flays. Impeccably folded. Like miniature sunsets. But. The staff over-bustled. Offered too much assistance. Especially this tall one. Kind of bony. Square face. And a harsh Slavic accent. She offered way more assistance than anybody wanted. Made me feel like a baby.

## Hula-Hoop

O. How she loved her roll-on deodorant. She rolled. And she rolled. She stood topless. In a half-slip. Before the mirror. And she rolled. She was good at the rolling. One small thing. She was good at. Anymore. (Should I be telling you this?) And then. Later. Bent over. Butt-naked. She clutched the tub. Waiting for help. My help. Indecorous. After 95 years. Of rigid propriety. I held on to her shoulders. So tiny. So gently. As if holding a sparrow. Or a butterfly. I held my inhale. Always had. Always did. She was pleated. She was huddled. In the tub. Like a victim. *Relax!* I said. *Cold!* She said. Angry! I felt stingy. It was summer. It was hot. I had the heat on! I was roasting. I was sweating. She wiped. With a washcloth. And a Dove bar. Under her surprisingly nice breasts. She wiped. And she wiped. *I feel dirty under there.* I just wiped her tiny back. I had nothing to say. I just wiped. I felt guilty. I was thinking of Shakespeare. As I watched her. She was folding. Into smaller and smaller pieces. Butt-naked. I turned away. And I looked in the mirror. O. My neck. O. Still holding up. My head. O. Still floating above the waves. My best memories. Spinning hula-hoops. Wearing crop-tops. Floral jams. Bellies tan. But. Then. They punched me. In the guts. (The mean ones.) And I cried. I cried hard. With no sound. That was hard. I had to hide it. I hid it.

## 2. Red

Mounds. Sounds. The plump. Rich lips. Allowed. To mount. The bold. The bloat. The tongue. A lick. A love. A loathing. Lust. To suck. The ripe. Tomatoes. Melons. Berries. Beets. Pang. Clang. Rough. Tough. Gooey. Crimson. Rims of round.

## Toothpicks

My mother detested. My father's toothpick habit. (I can understand.) How he probed. How he poked. Histrionically. High up in his mouth. Spitting gristle. On the tablecloth. *Vile*. That's what my mother said. Served us disgust. In the bowls of stewed tomatoes. From the San Joaquin Valley. He grew them. Tomatoes. And carrots. Milo maize. That shiny-faced Jew. From the Bronx. Who was starving. For cowboy. And farmer. For spaces. And stallions. For fanfare. And yachts. For oysters. And sweetbreads. For Cadillacs. Manicures. Big-bellied. Had it. For a second. Then. Lost it. Got it for a second. Then. Lost it. Too mad. Too mean. Unlucky. He could only hold on. To the cars. Always older. A little gaudy. A gold '62 Coupe de Ville. A '59 El Dorado. Lavender. Then. After he died. My mother took to toothpicks. Took a toothpick. Every meal. Worked it big. Picked big. Like the rest of us. *More things seem to stick to my teeth*. She'd say. We'd nod. And pick. We'd pick high. In search of gristle. From the brisket. Soggy celery strings. All our lips would stretch out. Like broken umbrellas.

## Day 33,002

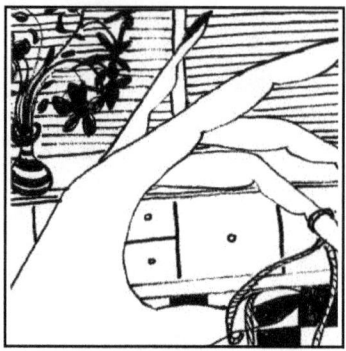

It was ugly. My mother's leg wound. Though. Not as ugly. As what was there. To begin with. Her doctor. Chinese. Dr. Ng. I liked her. Graceful muscles. And movement. Balletic fingers. And wrists. But. That leg wound. Got infected. Bared its teeth. All pus-y. The doctor ripped out the stitches. She scoured out the wound. Then. Stitched it up. With black twine. The wound was ugly. It was irate. Its mouth was hollering. The hole. About the size of a Mazda Miata. I spread ointment. Wrapped gauze. The wound finally began to close. Its lips pursed. *Your leg is healing.* I said. *The wound is getting smaller. It is?* She asked. *Are you kidding?* I said. *Tuesday it was the size of Detroit.* My mother laughed. Looked smug. Faced down another one. Barely a hitch. Day 33,002.

# Hat Story
## (in five parts)

1. Now. I wear his blond beret. The one he wore. Right before the end. With his turquoise string tie. A French cowboy. Caught in the holding pen. Outside Death's rodeo. A convalescent hospital. Where he died. With all those one-legged men. Roaring. Snoring. Crazed women who growled. Brains like cheese. Short quick nurses. From Manila. Then. He died.

2. I found his Lions' club pin. So. I pinned it to the edge of his champagne beret. Rides right above my eyebrow. Where he kissed me. Rare times. Like a whisper. In the 50s. Gray fedoras. In the 60s. White Stetsons. Then. Berets in the 70s. Berets in the 80s. Silly golf hats in the 90s. Kerchiefs like Gary Cooper. Ascots like David Niven. Groupings of medallions. Like Elvis going down.

3. My father's dead now almost 14 years. I never wear his red beret. The size of a pizza. Makes me feel like a clown. With a pie on my head. But. I wore it to his funeral. I remember him in it. More than the others.

4. I took all his hats. Nobody wanted them. Mostly berets. In the end. The white one. The green one. The blue one. The red one. The champagne.

5. No. There weren't any black ones. No gray ones. No brown. Those are the colors of my husband. Tweed tams. No. There weren't any tams. No. My father. He wasn't a tam man. No tweeds. No plaids. (Jews don't wear that much plaid.) No. I did not marry my father.

## Marital Clamp

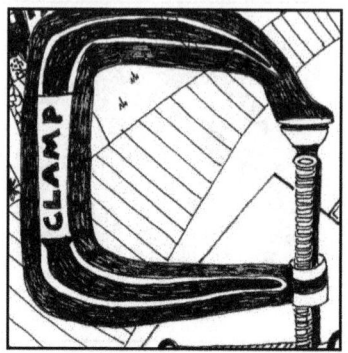

Sometimes. The jaws of a marriage. Grow tight. So tight. They clamp. Industrial strength. Yes. This happens. Every marriage. And if the marriage says it doesn't. This cramping. It's lying. You can verify. Is the TV on? Husband drinking scotch? Neat? Both bellies lying soft? On their groins? Like a baby? Are their bellies? Like a baby? Lying soft on their groins? Is she eating the fat? On the meat? Is she knitting thick textural scarves? By the dozens? Do her thumbs ache? Do her top teeth now fit like a tongue? In the groove of her bottom? Did she chisel the groove? With her clench? (While he slept.) Are her jawbones too loud? Are they louder than the snoring? Can you hear them? While she's driving down Powell? To work? Does he turn on some old Leonard Cohen? Does she turn on some old Leonard Cohen? Without knowing. Is that good?

## Rules of Marriage

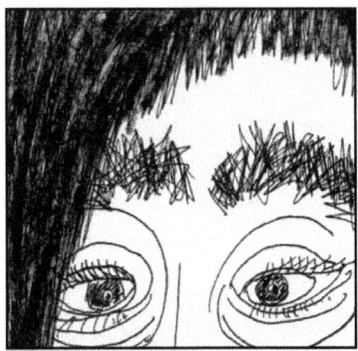

Soften fists. Straighten toes. Flex feet. Relax feet. Twist and shout. Unhump toes. Soften fists. Keep control of own damn socks. Shit freely. Close the door. Twist and shout. Have manners. Groom well. Be elegant. Point upwards. Point outwards. Open legs. Toes out. Flex feet. Twist and shout. Clip your toenails. Open chest. Allow eyebrows. Untuck blankets. Stop obeying. Laugh at eyebrows. Try obeying. Tame the basement. Clean the toaster. Rid crap. Surprise each other. Unhood everything. Surprise each other. Trust the children. Copy the dog. Lick the husband.

# 3. Purple

Velvet capes. And bodices. Skirts and drapes. So fat with folds. A man could choke. An aubergine deluge. Thick rabbit stews. Fresh beets that dye the broth. And fingertips. Of course. Like blood. A roasted boar. With wild berries. Eggplants. Bruises. Throats. Debauched. Such ugly royal brooches. Children squirm in churches. Next to aunties. Southside. Sunday hats. Like boulevards. Lit up for Jesus. Plums. I tell you. Eat the plums.

# Flash

After my father died. We went through his jewelry box. (I already told you.) The box was gorgeous. Carved mahogany. Curvaceous silver inlays. He bought it in Brazil. 1952. Sheen like a coffee bean. Sat on his dresser. Like a judge. Serious. Long brown robes. Played "Younger than Springtime." (Still does.) That time. In Brazil. She sambaed. My mother. In open-toed sling-backs. Crimson toenails were peeking. Through small gold-rimmed openings. Back at home. I was a baby. Hanging with Miss Tripp. An old nurse. She wore a nurse hat. And a nurse dress. And white leather shoes. With thick frightening soles. Thick as bigotry. Miss Tripp. Thin as chips. But the jewelry box? Bursting with man-jewels. Medallions. And belt buckles. Big chunky pieces. Like Cadillacs. Brazen behemoths. In *Mexican colors*. That's what my mother said. *Mexican colors*. That's what my father liked. *Mexican colors*. Flaming orange neck scarves. And hot pink berets. I liked it. His flash. I was his flash. For a long time. But. Afraid. We were both. Of each other. To begin with. And heights. And mediocrity. Especially mediocrity. It was awkward. He yelled. I flinched. I yelled. He kept yelling. I kept flinching. Until the end. He used to think. I was the smartest. The best hope. But then later. I was the dumbest. I felt the same. About him. Ditto. I hate to say.

**Blame**

For a long time. I thought it was. Her fault. Not mine. I mean. My mother's. Not mine. No. Yes. Everything. Then. One day. I knew. It was mine. Yes. Broke open. Like an egg yolk. But still. If it hadn't. Been mine. No. My mother's. To begin with. No. Wait. The way he screamed. Machines in our ears. Enormous anvils. The way he taught us. To scream. It might be his fault. I'm sifting. I'm cupping. I'm scooping through air. Slapping air. My hand's exhausted. My whole arm's exhausted.

**Piano Teacher**

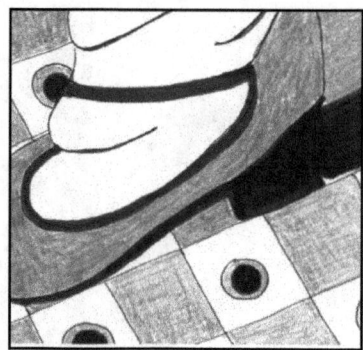

Big lady. BIG. And barrel-breasted. Buttoned into wrinkled linens. Yellowed along the edges. Like old newspapers. We were surrounded by glass cases. Dust on all glass. Dust on all bones. Bones lying on doilies with heart-breaking stitchery. Dying all over again. She had fingers like pouches. And feet. Like brown sacks. Gasp. Deep coughs of cologne. Giant vases of irises. Dead for two weeks. Such sad drag queens. I wait for my daughter. I remember a dress. That I wore in fifth grade. Velvet bodice. And an empire waist. It was purple. Like irises. Like dead irises. And Sally Berg's magnificent canopy bed. My first love. That bed. Of my life. I had French heels dyed to match.

## 4. Brown

Bread. O. Shanks. And short ribs. Planks of satiation. Sacs of fannies. Yeasted rumps. Gilded chews. O. Crusted chumps. O. Dads. O. Daddys. Square-torsoed papas. In chocolate brown slacks. Warm pillows of chest fur. Dark cordovan brogues. Burnished. Umber. Almond. Caramel. Chestnut. Flesh. O. Wood. O. Dirt. Dirty. Dirt.

**German Judges**

*Marriage is madness.* I uttered. Low moans like a mare. As I stared. Bumpy dunes of them. Large leather shoes. Then. I growled at him. Husband. I turned from him. Husband. Next day. I felt guilty. Made cocoa. Baked fig cake. O. Figs. O. Those bellies. Then. Early. Next day. Robins braided long lint threads. My husband sucked sap. From the sycamore trees. With his mouth. He massaged my tight neck. Massaged my old knees. Then. I sat at my desk. Let the ink swim through freely. Right through my fingertips. Dammit. God dammit. The neighbors came home. Started chainsaws. Demolished the hush. On the sidewalk. A long row of judges. From Germany. Stolid. And stoic. Like statues. With glasses on. Sat there and judged. Holding sleek ballpoint pens. They wore suits brown as shoes. And their jackets. All wrinkled and damp-looking. *Greek men invented the lie.* Said one fat one with invisible lips. He was right. And I sat there. Remembering. Picking my cuticles. Peeling my thumb skin. I waited. For scores. Hopeful. Not confident.

### The Enemy Is My Age

Ayman al Zawahri. Al Qaeda *mucky-muck*. Only six weeks older than me. Damn. That's depressing. I thought I'd be younger than the enemy. Didn't you? Is that what I look like? A landscape of dunes? Sling of chin hairs. Vast forehead. Like Asia. Too much forehead. For a face. And that chaotic corrugation. Of veins. Me. And Ayman. Bulby noses. Shiny snouts. Long thick sniffers. With spines veering right. Nostrils hidden. But. His eyes. Like old bullet holes. Flat. Black. Mean. Like ire. Or cancer. My eyes are much lighter. They are brown. Golden brown. Like a California foothill. Or a caramel pudding. My eyes have windows. Let in light. Right?

# Bees

My mother was. I repeat. A bird. Scaffolds of bird bones. The rest of us? Buttocks like yams. She fluttered. We trodded. A mini-deck of cards. Curtains hummed. In the ruffle of her whirr. But. She stuck. Like a barnacle. To Time. (Won't we all?) It's so obvious. Grasping my bicep. With everything she had. The last buoy. Right before the Final Undertow. Her legs kicked. And kicked. Like a toddler's. Until the end. The Very End. Wearing babydoll pajamas. Puffy sleeved. Dotted Swiss. Celery green. Her skin. Scattered with blotches. An artless map of continents. In every shade of brown. Not a lick. No. Not a lick. Of stillness to her. Never was. Even young. And plump. Her lap. At its most tranquil. And generous. A motor. Hive of bees.

## A Little Hip

I saw her. This morning. That woman. Who hunches. Who scuds. That woman. With the low brown dance. Then. I saw her. In the stacks. It was Tuesday. Late April. Brilliant outside. Babies. Bosoms. Blossoms. Blabber. But. That woman. As if aching. As if fielding a stoning. Without a fight. It enraged me. I want her open. I want her stronger. I want to tether her shoulders back. Like a turkey. Not to hurt her. Or scare her. Not to eat her. To make her bolder. I want her mighty. Plump and lungeing. Chest out. And I want her to rumba. Cha cha. Kick a little. I want some fingerpop. A little hip. Hey. Lady. Let the lizards scud.

# 5. Blue

Fathom blue. Fathoms of blue. Spectrums of blue. Sapphire. Cerulean. Clarity. Honesty. Density. Pockets of droop. Dirty workers. In denims. Exhausted. The tailors. The toilers. The maids. And the maintenance men. O. Swim into it. Blue. Swim into the dismal. The naughty. Unbuttoned. The bruises. The choking. Sink into it. Dive. Now get out. Now envision the order. Tiny buttons. Like spines. Down her blouse. Prissy lips. Fathom proof. And protection. Calming chords. In minor progressions. Fathom slanted. Folded anger. Fathom stacks. Fathom phlox. Fathom meadows of cornflowers. O. Magnificent sky. Fly right into. Aquamarine. Float right into it. Float. Come on. Float.

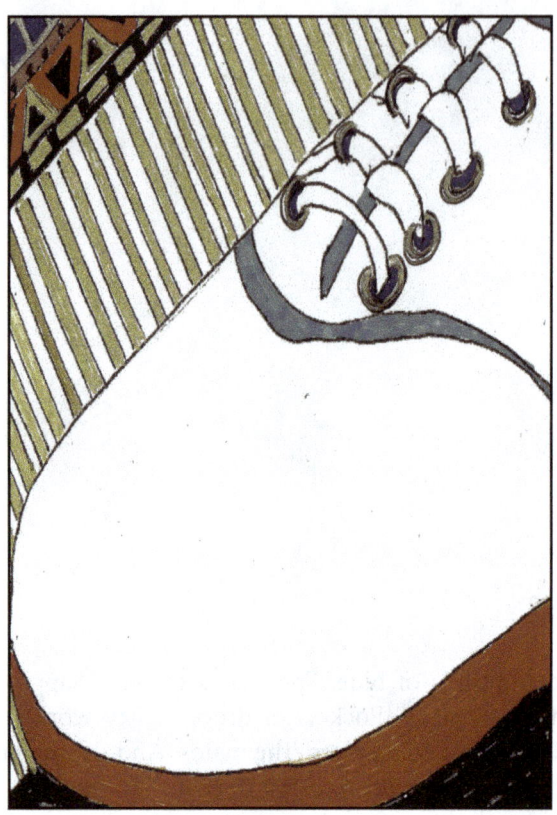

**Sheen**

At 90. She leapt. Into a Venetian flatboat. As if one of the Flying Wallendas. Right off the street. Over the wobbling canal. But. She had to. Make the leap. We had to. Catch the boat. Phew. She aced it. Not a hitch. In her Triple-A Keds. They were yellowed. Like teeth. After so many washings. How she'd worried. For months. *Hey. You got this.* We said. *Piece of cake.* Then. She nailed it. Boom. Cruising. On the ripples. To the airport. Her face shone. *You know.* She said. *Most of my friends. They can't even walk.* She was staring. At the moon. We were staring. At the moon. And her face shone. Yes. Brilliant against the sky. Yes. Her sheen. Outshone the moon's. And the Adriatic's. Sheen for sheen. My mother's face.

## Pinkie Ring

I never saw him wear it. The sapphire pinkie ring. But there it was. Curled up. And glowing. Like a secret kiss. Next to his Hebrew medallions. Gold Stars of David. Chais on thick chains. Monogrammed cufflinks. And. Belt buckles. Crafted from huge hunks of Oregon myrtlewood. Chunky turquoise bolo ties. My father's jewelry. It slept in that beautiful wood box. Atop the mahogany highboy. Like a mountain. He was ready to die. He kept talking to his mother. *Mama.* He would say. *See you soon.* (Yes. It cracked me open.) Sifting through his jewelry. That sapphire pinkie ring. Fit me like elastic. Left hand. Middle finger. I liked it. It looked good. Until one day. I looked down. I was bleeding. At the ring. So. I moved it. Right hand. Index finger. It spun a little. Made me worry. Then. One year. I lost it. Then. I found it. In a glove. The band is silver. Worn soft. Like an old '45. The stone is absolute blue. Endless blue. The blue of answers. There are six tiny diamond chips. Sometimes. I hear them singing. They are sitting before mirrors. At tiny vanities. All sopranos. They sound like Tinkerbell. Later. They listen. And remember things. The sapphire always feels warm. Even when my fingers are frigid.

### The War of 2001
*September 13, 2001*

I told my new therapist. She was concerned. I was not feeling. The tremendous storms of grief. Bolts of grief. The glut. The spate. The jolts. The coats of grief. I told her. "What?? I wake up early. Every morning. Make a stack of hotcakes. For the wolves of fear. Then. Sit an hour. Feeling! Hard-backed wooden chair. First cold. Then hot. Then cold. My legs folded under. Like paperclips. Sit there. Staring. All the pictures. Like gray checkers. In the *New York Times*. With catchy headlines. All the women. Desperate women. With their messy ponytails. And lustrous fingernails. That clutch their largest photos. Of their smiling sons. And men. Now dust. To dust. In pretty hands. Like flags of surrender. Cry," I said. "I cry. Just cry and cry. My old knees screaming for relief. I can't release them. Make immediate plans. For yoga."

My new therapist smiled warmly. With her ample crooked mouth. Then. Adjusted her large stomach. Though I tried to not. I stared. "Good." She said. "That's good." Next time. I thought. I have to tell her. I've been crying. Just this way. For years. The tears embedded. In my sad and ancient code. "But still," I say. "My God. This time," I say. "We've really done it. Etched the membrane. Set the branding. Look. It's on the faces. Even babies. Look. Like scarecrows. Ankles. Sharp. And poking. Out their bright white shoes. I mean. I mean. The white men cry. That's big." I say. Next time. I'm going to have to. Tell her. Only seconds can I. Actually feel each day. Or I might die. Like them. By the horrible weight of it.

O. I felt so strong. At first. I shouldered. Quite a bulk of it. Then. My muscles burned. My scalp grew tight. Oh. Gandhi. Can you hear me? Gandhi. Can you hear me?

## Growing Smaller

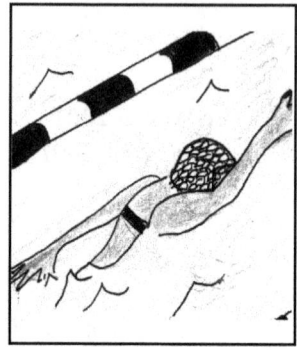

Conked my forehead. Metal door. 24-hour Fitness. Hollywood District. Portland. Oregon. 3:35 AM. Awake since 2:05. Tried to sleep. 73 minutes. Whirred like an eggbeater. Puréed sheets. Finally. Got up. (What a relief.) Put on bathing suit. Drove to gym. Conked forehead. Locker door. Didn't notice. Jimmied on cap. Scalp hurt. Looked in mirror. Trickle of blood. Loping down cheek. Like teenage boy. Pants post-ass. Boxers poofing. Thoughts of my mother. Her look of devastation. On her face. At the devastation. Of her face. When she dared to look. At her face. I patted the wound. Put pressure on its lips. Then. Strode to the pool. Wore my thighs. Like corduroy knickers. (As usual.) Pool was mine. Glory. Hallelujah. All mine. Pool was still as a sidewalk. O. Damn. One guy in the Jacuzzi. Comfortable face. Like a suede chair. Two medallions. Glinting. Glinting. Off his plump chest. I dove in the pool. Loved up the liquid. Gliding. Gliding. Became smaller. And smaller. So small.

**Family Cruise after the Dad**

We gathered. On a boat. We swayed. And swirled. Especially the elders. We tiptoed. Hesitated. Separated. Hid. Squirmed. Shrugged. Hugged. Hobbled. Ate. Burped. Laughed. Got up. Sat down. Swam. Ate. Drank. Got up. Sat down. Scrubbed. Wiped. Swam. Wiped. Put on cologne. Rarely went limp. Exercised. Exercised. Tried to decipher. Tried. Tried. Churned. We churned. Growled. Yearned. Took on a tone. Confessed. Regressed. There was restlessness. Cocktails. Cocktails. We floated. We avoided the screaming. His screaming. Embroidered in our membranes. No screaming. There was laughter. There was breathing. There was flat-handed touching. There was familial pride. There were cocktails. And nibbles. There was care. There were powerful curves.

### Do Birds Tumble in The Forest?

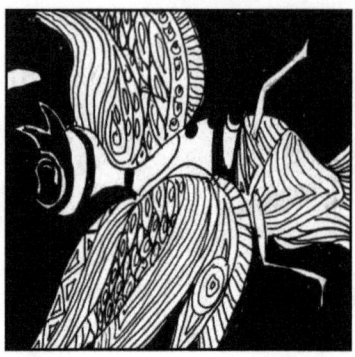

O. Birds. How they fall into it. Float into it. Swoop into it. Swoon. The cosmic respiration. We try. To glide. Get snagged. Get scared. We clutch. We grasp. We stick. And stiffen. Look at them. Hookless. Do birds ever tumble? Do they love fermented berries? Do they love them too much? Are there avian addicts? Procedures in place? Is there treatment? Is there ADHD? Do they ruin their voices? Did they get that from us? Do they ever forget? How to fly? How to nest? Did they get that from us? Is there PTSD?

# 6. Gray

Humble. Slender. Tall. Quiet. An artful roar. Of silent might. Blur. Fuzz. Indistinction. Immortality. Pencils. Shadows. Chronic detachment. Muting. Bad muting. Passive. Implications. Gusts. Dusts. Dirty snow. Timid pewter. Pavement. Pebbles. Portland. Pleats. Plaids. Vests. Lint. Loss. Convention. Sallow. Pallors. Ashen. Sweaters. Wools. Blends. Hues. Warmth. Irish sheep.
Baa.                              Baa.

# Math Strain

I started touring my brain. All sides. Checking it out. Left side in particular. It used to be. Quite remarkable. Shored up. (That inherited math strain.) Ruled for years. But. I damned it. Got tired of its being so tidy. I dove into the eddies. Instead. On the other side. To the right. Swirled for years. Then. I was wondering. Does it work over there? To the left. Anymore. It's so dusty. Disgusting. I remember it spotless. And agile. Posture impeccable. Folding and stacking. Folding and stacking. (It remembers itself.) But my left brain's been chillin'. Eatin' Ben & Jerry's. Watching "Grey's Anatomy." Left brain's grown flabby. It farts when there's company. It laughs so much longer. And louder. Than it should. Now. My left brain just annoys people. Looks like an over-stuffed husband. In an over-stuffed chair.

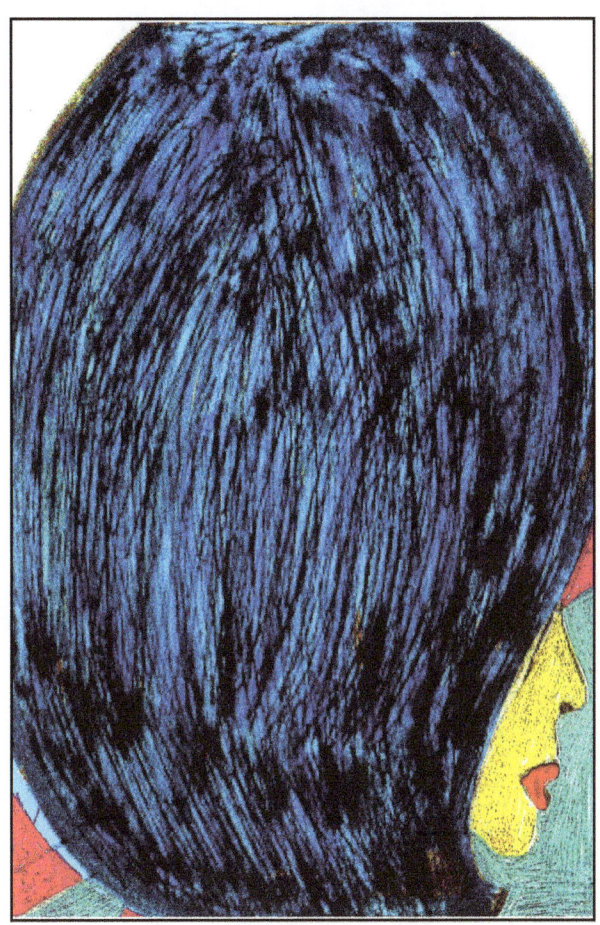

**Another Hair Story**

At 95. She stopped coloring her hair. Let it go gray. Like gravel. Like any old gramma. In her youth. My mother's hair. Black as patent leather shoes. Like my father's. And my brother's. And mine. Not my sister's. Hers was orange. Like a crayon. Eyes like fresh key lime pie. I was jealous. Of her colors. But. My mother's hair. Black. Like kalamatas. Then auburn. Like tamari almonds. Then brown. Bronze. Then golden blonde. Then strawberry blonde. Apricot. Champagne. Until last year. Gray. Like a Weimaraner. Round as a melon. Her caregiver set it in rollers. Every Saturday. She had a stand-up dryer. My mother's hair looked better than ever. It was puffy. It was always way puffier than mine. (I liked puffy. She liked puffy.) My mother had twice as much hair. As I ever will.

**Romance**

In my own private bootcamp. Militaristic crossburn. It's a mental strand. Abrasive. Internally. Aggressive. Internally. Yet. Buttoned. Enough! I'm revolting. Going truant. Going vocal. External. I'm looking. Outwards. I'm being earnestly visual. My eyes pointed outwards. (I tied up and gagged my own tyrant.) New directive. Live outwards. At the pIayground. For instance. A tennis ball sat there. Gray as Disinterest. Soggy. Alone. In the grass. I kicked it. Across the lot. Right into the brambles. It came to rest. Right against another tennis ball. Soggy. As gray as slacks. Two old tennis balls. Touching each other. Soft. Round hip. To soft round hip.

## Fresco

At first. It looked like dog bones. That's what I thought. Petrified canine skeleton. Creepy. Etched into the banks of the Washougal. Right where I swam. Seconds before. Such a precise imprint. Arced ribcage. Angled leg bones. Snouty jaw. Susan got close. She named it. *Deer. It's deer bones.* I was spooked. By the death of it. Fled. Then. I breast-stroked back slowly. And gazed at its artistry. *Magical.* Lanny said. *A blessed omen.* BUT ROTTING DEAD DEER STERNUM MEMBRANE MAY HAVE BRUSHED UP AGAINST MY BATHING SUIT. I shouted dramatically at Lanny. Only half in jest. THAT DEER'S LAST LIVING LUNG CELL MIGHT BE WATER IN MY EAR. I swam quickly back to shore. I cleared that thing. By at least fifty yards. It was later. Years later. I. Finally. Grew the balls. To see a ghost.

# 7. Black

So egotistical. Yet. Essential. So self-satisfied. So self-contained. So selfish. Stereotypical. Effortless. Uniform. Within. Inside. Beyond. Below. Under. Over. Older than anything. Darker than anything. Pits. Prunes. Seeds. Olives. Ooh. Boo. Eek.

## Underarm Hair

I remember. That day. I was 12. Like a spire. In my armpit. Black. Against the smooth golden mesa. Of my childhood. A Nigerian. In Iceland. Portent of a four-decade invasion. Coarse. Black. Fecund. And now. Fifty years past. Scant. A motley crew. In silent retreat. A toss of threads. Still. Black as coal. I send out scouts. Few hairs to report. Perhaps. They've entered a Witness Protection Program. Or. I imagine them retired. Kickin' it. In Boca. Yeah. Boca Raton. With the Levys. The Bergs. And the Julius Cohens.

**Tiny Writers**

It was hot. Heat galloped over me. Prancing. Wahoo. Yippee-Ky-Ay. Cowboys could have grilled flapjacks. On my shoulders. Cinnamon ferns inked shadows. Complex coils. Almost Victorian. On the walls. It was lovely. I went out. Watched the wind fluff oak's bouffants. Then. Knelt in the garden. Such as it were. One small tomato. Four tongues of basil. Then. We cut down that cherry tree. Sick as a dog. And the light came back. After 25 years. I knelt in the garden. Combed out the dirt. With my fingertips. Tried to decipher. Two cigarette butts. One curled-up fruit label. One pink bread tag. Two dried-up tulip bulbs. A small square of black plastic. A beetle's tablecloth. An earthworm's serape. And hundreds of ants. Marching. Along the edges. Of everywhere. Perhaps. I thought. They will write tiny novels. About stink bugs. And beetles. And earthworms. And other ants. On counters. In cabinets. Corners. And cake crumbs. Their misfortunes. Smashings. And swattings. The numerous tragedies. Ants handwrite. In tiny journals. Their penmanship is excellent. They write in cursive. (They did not learn it in school.)

## Thicketry

But something ropey. In the way. Between. My mother and me. A sliver-giving thicketry. I got scratched. She got scratched? Every time. We edged closer. Got tangled. In history. Dusty maze. I was mad at her. Sixty-four years to get over it. Back then. She stiffened her arms. Held her arms. Way too close. To her body. For a mother. (In my opinion.) Way too thin. Bored by food. For a mother. We were hungry. For bakery. For French fries. And skin. We grew mean. And she sniffed me. *Head smells.* Sniff. Sniff. Still. I am eating too much. Can I ever get over it? Hope so. I think. Yes. I slipped on my gloves. And entered the thicket. Time. Shit. Already out the door. At the end. Only. I forgave her. I saw her. I held her. I kissed her.

## My Generous Collar

I was emailed a poem. The other day. By David Lehman. I liked it. I printed it. I put it in my pocket. There was an image. A piano. *Rank & file/Black & white.* A good way to describe a piano. I thought. Then. I went to see my father. He was sleeping. In his deathbed. A tube. Up his nose. A tube. Down his throat. It had a headlamp. A camera. A feeler. What was snorting down there? Everyone was asking. All the busy doctors. Sifting through the ashes. Thousands of fat cigars. Towers of salami. Their casings. Stacked like undershirts. Vats of butter. And margarine. Vats of chicken fat. Bullets of anger. Dunes of anguish. The green gravy of disappointment. Last time I saw him. I wore a generous collar. Expensive white blouse. Ruffled. Liquid. Fit like a bath. But. I felt like a turtle. Or a cowgirl. I sat on his deathbed. And stared. I stared dry-eyed. Lock-jawed. A vast devastation. Put my hand on his arm. Mottled with blotches. Hip touching hip. Sat on his deathbed. Still. For the first time. Read him the poem. By David Lehman. He smiled. He liked it. He liked the piano. His eyes closed. His life force was eddying. Down the Final Drain. He was smiling. Days later. He died. Alone. I was driving North on I-5. My mother was driving South on Pershing. Heading to the cleaners. Picking up that fancy blouse.

## Onus

And still. The days of the hair shirt. Slavic overcoat. Loaded. With load. Big slash pockets. Stuffed. And sagging. With sandbags. My head drops. To the right. My neck crackles. Drops left. It sticks. Tight as catgut. Muscles groan. Their groans frighten me. Frighten the neighbors. The neighbors retaliate. With chainsaws. They chainsaw their hawthorns. They chainsaw their shrubbery. O. Such a high wretched screaming. I curse at my neighbors. And out the door. I put on my ugliest slippers. And hate. There's an ear-splitting hiss. I just hate. Wear my hot robe of shame.

## Sunday 4 AM

Hush. It's the opposite of blasts. The opposite of bombings. The opposite of any kind of offensive. No greed. No roar. No screech. No Trump. On Sunday. 4 AM. I'm up. As always. The rat race. On recess. The motors are off. The heater is brushing its teeth. And deep-stretching. Dust sambas with fruit flies. The sofas are ironing their skirts. Snores and farts. Snores and farts. Sloppy giants. Are bumbling about. Newspapers softshoe. Up onto the porches. In their angular jackets. They are thin as Fred Astaire. No one would conceive of mowing his lawn. No leaf-blowers. It's the opposite of blowhards. And trucks. Nothing's self-conscious. Not even Sunday. Soft bakers shape scones. The loveless weep evenly. Into silk pillows. The damaged are stalking their prey. Yes. The wolves howl. Eerily. Far in the distance. Like in Akron, Ohio. Where Jan sleeps. No doubt. (She could sleep through anything.)

# 8. Green

Kiwis. Soft as Christmas bodices. Mists of limes. Slinks of cukes. Envy. Stains. And grudges. Dairy fungus. Peas. And pears. And pippin apples. Sinewy biceps of celery. Flounces of spinach. Beans. Beans. Caterpillars. Caterpillars. Slide-step on lawns. Capes of lawn. Ferns. And forests. And flora. Fecundity. Flap jackets. Peridots. Pistachios. Malachite. Meadows. Mint. Snot. Goo. Fresh guacamole. Honeydew melons. Casabas. O. Casabas.

**Wood Clothes**

I've always been jealous. Jealous of you. Jealous of your hair. Your height. Your legs. Your feet. Your eyes. The green in your eyes. The blue. Jealous of your red satin skirts. Your purple satin skirts. Your soft velvet bodices. Tartans and tinsel. (As a Jew.) I was jealous of your creamy. Your chenille. Yes. Your Easter. I coveted your hats. Big straw hats. Like a garden umbrella. Roses and lilies and daffodils. Giggles of baby's breath. Snapdragons. Lightshows of ribbons. So jealous of your five-pointed stars. Your swags of wee lights. All the twinkling. O. Jealous of your soft buxom mothers. Who baked and who fried. O. I wanted the pork chops. So jealous of your angels. And strange explanations. Not jealous of your fish sticks. Forget it. And frankly. Your churches. Forget it. Admittedly gorgeous. Beyond beyond belief. (So to speak.) But. I'm allergic. To churches. They give me an itch. They make me feel. Just like I'm wearing wood clothes. Gigantic rough wood clothes. It feels awful.

**Not Another Shoe Poem**

She matched. Top half matched. Her bottom half matched. Her head. Waistline. Thighs. Calves. Belts. Shoes. Purses. Jewelry. Matched. Clasps? Matched. It was deliberate. Everything. Well-put-together. Everyone said. Dozens of lipsticks. Hundreds of tones. Ninety minutes easy. Every day. Putting on face. Getting hair done. Every Friday. Fingernails. Toenails. Such lovely feet. Triple-A width. Slender and pale. Yes. Feet looked like doves. Funny. She was always trying. To give me her shoes. *I can't wear them.* I'd say. I'd been saying it for years. *My feet are round. And stubby. Like potatoes.* She'd laugh. In her closet. Many stacks of skinny shoes. Original boxes. Carefully labeled. KELLYGREEN HEELS. NAVY BUCKLE FLATS. CHERRYRED KEDS. FANCY SILVER PUMPS. EVERY LETTER WAS A CAPITAL. Slanted. Sometimes with a serif. She had a drawer. Spilled with scarves. Exquisite fluid angels. Yet. Her body. The opposite. Choppy. Restless. Detached. Her fingers were cold. Sharp. Her bracelets jangled. My daughters. Thank god. My daughters. They're here. Like fires. They flare. They flared. Over the both of us. Warmed us. Kissed us. Both. In time. On the mouth. My daughters. The good queens. They lifted us. In time. Cradled us. Spun us. My daughters. They rocked us. Rooted. My mother and me.

# Disclaimer

There was an enormous feature article. Friday paper. About one of my very best friends. Another performer. Director. Writer. Dancer. Mother. Kind. Generous. Friend. The article was about the size of an Oldsmobile. Lots of color photos. I got jealous. Shot pellets of vitriol. Like throwing beanbags. Through a clown nose. From the child's line. Next day. 3 AM. I worried. Hard. About my chronic storehouse of bile. Next day. My guts hurt. I kept folding. And unfolding. My legs. Then. I realized. I have fingernails. All over me. Still. And. Only too happy. To scratch.

**Felt**

Another dream. Yes. I'll keep it brief. Just as brief as the others. In the dream. My husband and I. We are falling. Together. Hand-in-hand. Through air. I am panicked. Face flat. Body taut. Eyes bulging. Eyebrows! Off the charts! *Don't worry.* He says. *We are falling into leaves. Into piles of soft leaves. We are falling through softness. Into softness. Onto leaves.* He says it softly. But. We realize. Together. We are falling. Into canyons. Rock canyons. Not leaves. Jagged canyons. Abysmal canyons. Hell's Canyon looks like crow's feet. Compared to these. We realize. Together. We will die. Skewered. Splintered. Shredded. Smashed. A terrible dream. *Wait!* My husband screams. *It's felt! The canyon's felt! It's made of felt.* I touch it. It's felt. We will live. I awake. Fast. I have to.

# 9. Yellow

A ray. A spray of gleam. A splay. A fizz arisen. Splish. Splash. A honk of blare. Blaze of flay. A vast display. The bright. Heat. Sweet. Quench. Burble. Babble. Effervescence. Farm cream. Ripe bananas. Lemon flesh.

## The Lemon and the Lama

The day the Dalai Lama came to town. I woke up jawing. A large wedge of lemon. Soul puckering. Flies were scratching their whiskers. Against the screen door. And the back door. Of my guts. I went to see him anyway. Taking less time. Than I normally would. With my hair.

The Dalai Lama stood grinning. From a plastic pagoda. In the middle of the square. I was standing on a bench. With a rare clear vision. There were thousands of people. They had gathered to behold him. There were mothers below me. They were handing me their children. Hoping I might field. Divine blessing. Like a Frisbee. There were wheelchairs and epidemics. There were Christians in a state of suspended bliss. There were Jews. Still waiting.

The Dalai Lama floated. Wearing robes of vivid berry. His left arm was pale and bare. I could see his curly pit hairs. They were black. Sparse. His lips were up. Like they were waving. Crinkly eyes. Like ragdoll stitches. Big. Uneven crinkles. The shiniest thread of sad. He said. *Peace is more than absence of violence.* He said. *Peace is also action.* He said. *Compassion grease the wheels.*

On the bike ride. Back home. Over the river. I couldn't get "Hello, Dolly," the song, out of my mind. I laughed. Laughed at everything. The whole way home.

**Personal Growth**

Before. Times past. I feared the crow's forebodance. The blackness. The legends. They panicked me. Rife. Sharp. Skinny like a cigarette. Shiny like a shoe. Flapping. Squawking. Picking. My skin crawled. But. Today. I saw one. A crow. As ballerina. Doing jêtés. And arabesques. In a tutu. Backyard crow. Sleek peacock. Regal beatnik. Today. A crow was Nureyev. Not the dirge piper. Yay.

The
Day
My
Mother
Died

Absolutely everything has been said about the death of the mother. It's enormous. It's bigger than a brontosaurus. It's like its own planet.

How in the end, the mother curls up like a fingernail or an apple stem on the coffee table. And how desperately sad that is. It's almost unbearable. Those bastard details of the body going down.

And yet, in the end, the body's brilliant. How its juices finally take control of the mind. When the throat no longer swallows. When the food and water stop. The organs spray out their personal opioids. And keep the dying stoned. So kind. The body as perfect host.

December 17. 2015. That's the day my mother died. Four days after her 97th birthday. (For which she was comatose. So. I'm not sure it counts.)

Rumi died on December 17. (My mother wasn't a poet.) The 13th Dalai Lama died on December 17. (I don't think she was exalted.) Cesaria Evora died on December 17. (My mother never went barefoot.)

My mother lay comatose for six days. Her little body a little cockeyed. Legs crossed. Toes pointed inward. Her hands were burning up. Holding the fever. Holding her hands. Holding the fever. In life. Her hands had been. Cold as cement. Like mine.

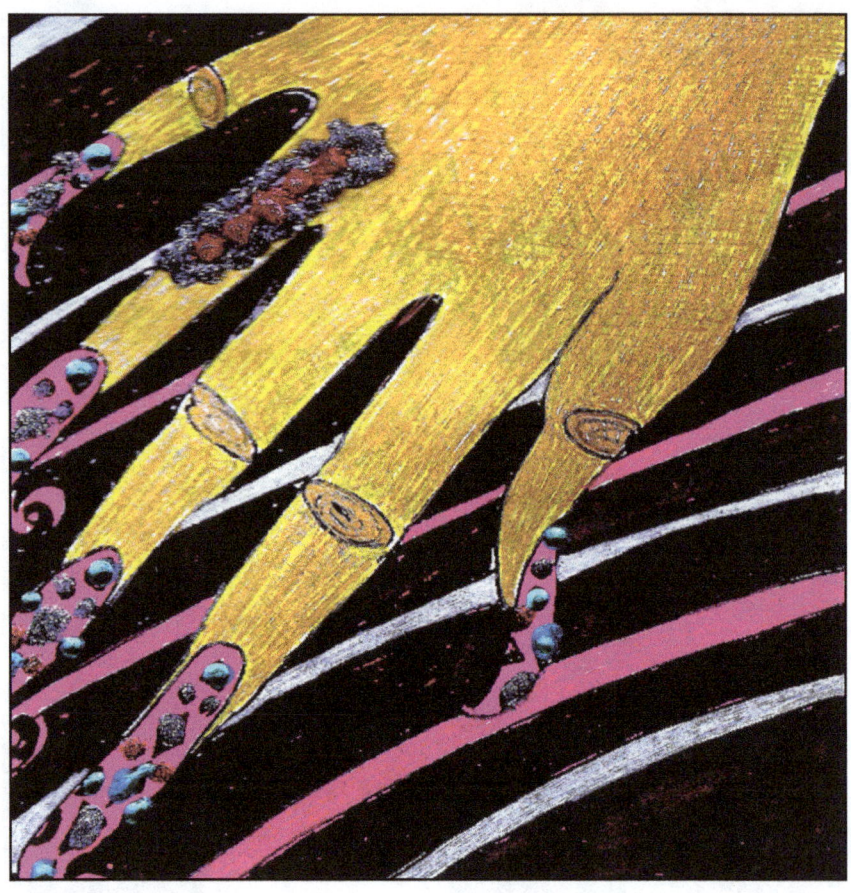

No one had clipped her toenails for weeks. They were curled under like Flo Jo's fingernails. My mother would have died if she saw them.

My mother's nurses were from Guatemala and Haiti. They kept tearing up. And telling me how funny my mother was. They all said she was so funny. I couldn't think of one joke. I couldn't think of one time when she was funny. I called my sister and my sister said Well, she wasn't funny to us. She just wasn't that funny.

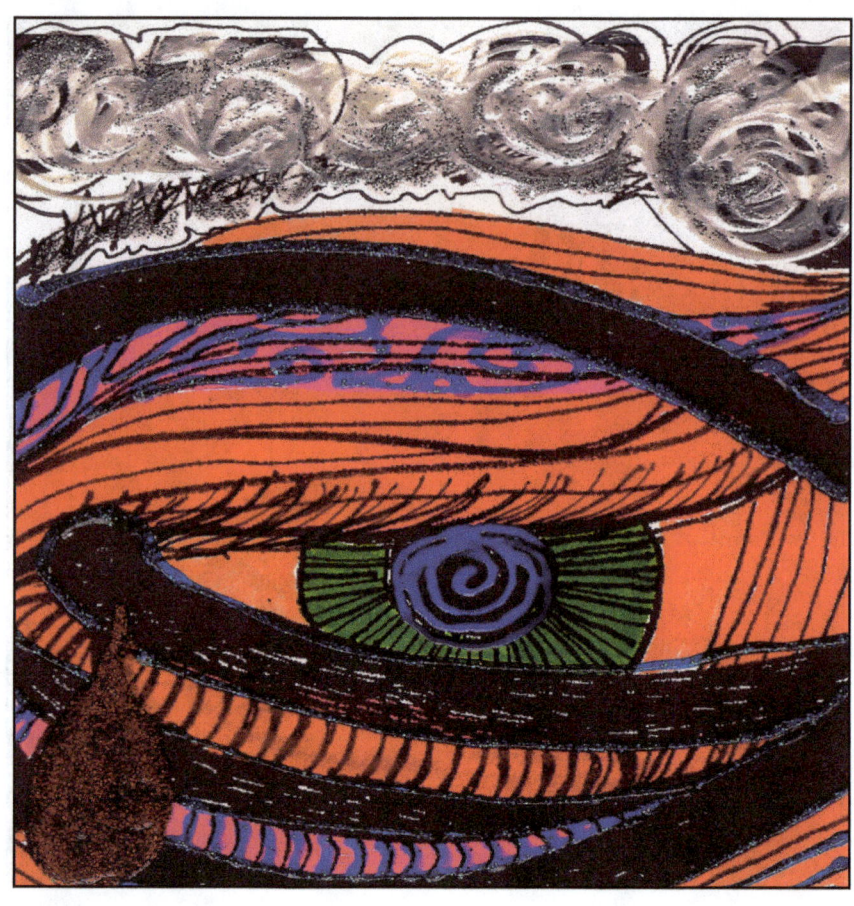

My mother had an eye infection for months. (Should I be telling you this?) The rim of her left eye was swollen and crimson. Like a young mouth. But on an old eye. It looked bloody awful.

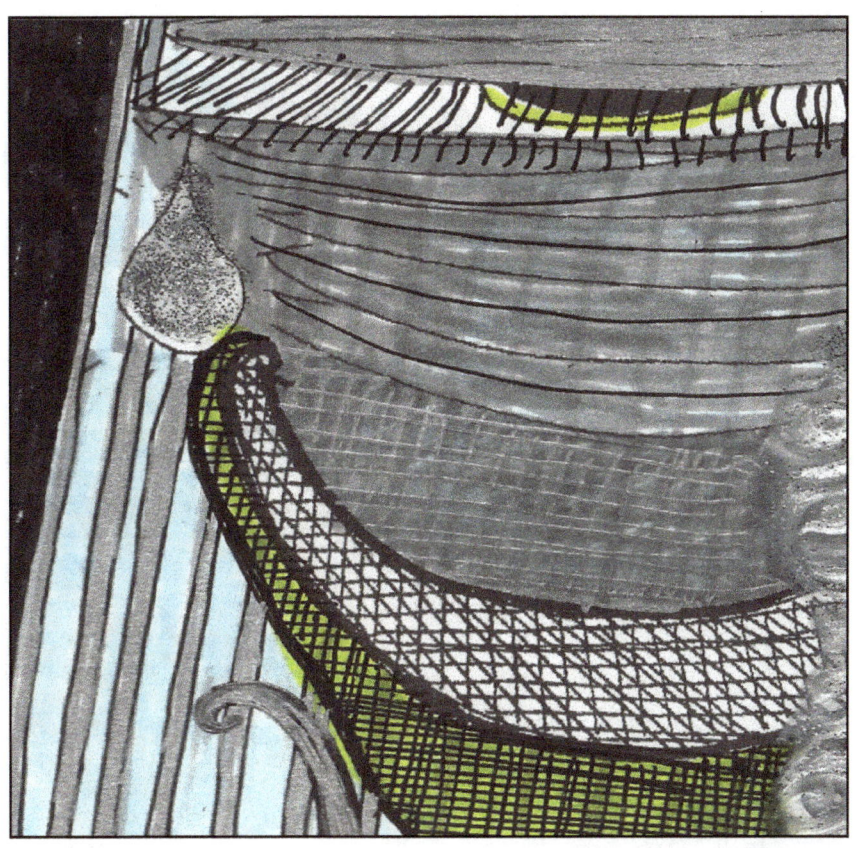

But the instant my mother died. The redness disappeared. And one clear tear fell. From the corner of her bad eye. Crystalline. Glimmering. Shimmering.

I could smell Death when Death came into her room. Death didn't smell fleshy. Not fleshy. Or fishy. More a rusty smell. Metallic. A fainter scent than I'd expected. Yet more nauseating. A ghost odor of something putrid.

My mother closed her mouth. And made a funny face. A comedian's face. Like Red Skelton or Jonathan Winters. Her lips curled under as if she were toothless. Which she wasn't. She had more teeth than I do. It wasn't a smile, exactly. But a contented look. *Okay. I'm done.* She seemed to say. *I'm out of here.*

Death looked like Richard Boone. Paladdin. Remember him? Pleated face. Black suit. Black hat. Little white teeth. He came at noon. On the dot. I offered him some caesar salad but he said he had to go. He was driving a '62 Porsche. Matte black. No muffler. It was obnoxious.

The End.

Leanne Grabel, M.Ed., is a writer, illustrator, performer and special education and language arts teacher (in semi-retirement). In love with mixing genres and media, Grabel has written and produced numerous spoken-word multi-media shows, including "The Lighter Side of Chronic Depression"; "Anger: The Musical"; and "The Little Poet." Her poetry books include *Flirtations; Lonesome & Very Quarrelsome Heroes; Short Poems by a Short Person; Badgirls* (a collection of flash non-fiction, as well as a theater piece); and most recently, *Assisted Living*, a chapbook of graphic prose poems. Grabel has just completed *Tainted Illustrated,* a graphic stretched memoir, which is being serialized in **THE OPIATE**. Grabel and her husband are the founders of Cafe Lena, the legendary Portland poetry cafe of the 90s. Grabel has two daughters, some fabulous sons-in-law, an itty bitty granddaughter Ophelia, and Bailey, the best dog ever.

www.ingramcontent.com/pod-product-compliance
Lightning Source LLC
Chambersburg PA
CBHW050528170426
43201CB00013B/2132